THE HUMAN USER
MANUAL

MARK NAGHSH LMSW CMC

CONTENTS

PREFACE

In today's world, we get licensed for things that impact safety and security for those around us. We get licensed to drive a car, practice medicine, provide therapy, etc. This requires studying and training, so we are well-equipped and prepared to face less than optimal situations.

We have many innate gifts and talents, but there are no manuals or guidelines on how to be our best via accessing our internal processing system. We get trained in C++ or Python programming. We learn English, but no one spends the time to teach us about our inner selves. In this book, we will look at different parts of ourselves through a clinical lens. We will break it down like an instruction manual to learn how to operate the complexity of being a human in the simplest manner possible.

Humans are born with the basic physiological components listed in the getting to know your device section, so we will not go through the specifics here. Our focus will mainly be on the operating system, which is your brain. As you know, your brain is an amazing tool that has developed over years of evolution and has unlimited possibilities. The basic structure includes the Forebrain, Midbrain, and the Hindbrain. The brain manages all aspects of your functioning, short-term and long-term processing, nervous system, emotional and automatic functioning such as breathing and heart rate. It is quite complex, so I will not break it down, but it sets us apart from all species on this planet. Knowing how it functions, this manual will remain in the areas within our control, such as Emotion, memory, and processing. The goal is to give you operating instructions based on your experiences so you can use them to improve your ability to engage in life and have more meaningful interactions with those you care about.

Controls and Display

Brain/CPU

- Runs both autotomic and manual functions such as respiration, digestion as well as thinking, speaking, processing, and calculations

Eyes

- They are the visual sensory devices that take in environmental factors and relay them to the brain

Mouth and Lips

- Seal the main orifice used for breathing and eating. They can also be used for talking, kissing, whistling, and making raspberry sounds

Nose

- Used for breathing, smelling, snoring, snorting, and holding device to enhance Eye vision ability

Ears

- Used for hearing and Balance as well as holding devices to improve Eye vision

Skin

- The protective layer prevents infection and injury.

CHAPTER ONE

Clinical Understanding

Clinical Knowing + Intuitive Knowing = Increased Insight

In writing a guide to the successful use of ourselves as a device through the lens of clinical understanding, you might ask, "What experience do you have that would be of value to me?" Well, experience is relative to the point of contact in this world. Human behavior, knowledge, and intuition are what really lead us to a true understanding of how we operate. This idea includes relationships, self-awareness, and interaction with the physical world. Without truly knowing ourselves, the ability to gain control of ourselves as human beings become a mystery. Our goal is to remove the mystery, so you engage your mind like any other operational tool

What separates the great leaders from the good and the good from the average? It comes down to a simple concept "know thyself". Without knowing ourselves, the ability to gain control and draw out the needs of the other remains an abstract concept filled with the distortions of our own needs and thereby reduces the percentage of positive interactions. Our brain should not be operating us, but we need to learn how to operate it. This is especially important when we interact with others.

In this manual, our challenge is to move forward with this new understanding to become a better relationships person and a more functional human being. These do not have to be mutually exclusive. Given that the CPU or brain filters all input devices, it is important to understand how our brains interpret information. Simply put, all information is based on previous experiences. We would all like to think we are unbiased or objective when it comes to this information, but we are not. Our past experiences impact how we take information, at a given instance, and how we react to them. This creates suggestions on how we engage, for we might be looking through a lens distorted by the brain's subjectivity, for everything is contextual with the brain, for it tries to make connections to assist us. For example, the brain can sort out misspelled words, and it even flips what we see right side up for the lens of our eyes see images upside down. By understanding this, you can gain a better understanding that you need to disconnect from what you think you know and start to look at what you do know. You will learn to gain operational control of a device that no one ever taught you how to use. This will help you understand your physiological responses to people, such as emotional arousal, physiological reactions, or compensatory behavior. Let's look at a few formulas that can assist us in these.

- Intuitive Knowing (what we feel is true) + Clinical Understanding (what our experiences tell us) = Increased Insight (what is really happening)
- Physical Knowing (Familiarized physical experience) + Insight (what is really happening) = Increased Empathy (understanding of what others may be going through understanding ourselves).
- Empathy (understanding of what others may be going through) + Spiritual Knowing (Separating the physical aspects of ourselves from the spirit to achieve an observing ego (God space) = Increased Positive Relationships

- Intuitive Knowing + Clinical Understanding = Increased Insight
- Physical Knowing + Insight = Increased Empathy
- Empathy + Spiritual Knowing = Increased Positive Relationships

Connections are not connections at all but the result of the relationship of Physical, Intuitive, and Clinical concepts. By analyzing these concepts, we can begin to tear down the pretense and see things as they are. We then have relational potential through the careful analysis of our social imprint via the lens of clinical understanding. This potential can be on an individual level or a larger group level. By gaining access to the language that drives the unconscious reaction, you will better understand how the brain will operate you versus you operating your brain.

Our clinical needs and expectations of a potential relationship are also connected to our brain's desire to make connections for us or resolve other issues, so it is important for us to be mindful when it does its own thing. By gaining an understanding of simple clinical concepts and defense mechanisms, you can thwart your brain's attempt to "fill in" the blanks for you. In this process, we will look at concepts such as

- Attachment Theory
- Object Relation Theory
- Counter-transference
- Jungian Archetypes

The goal is to connect these concepts directly to your interactions with others specifically. Our internal mechanisms that drive our interactions need some guide rails of understanding so you can identify them when you see and feel them manage your relational interactions better. Through varying levels of interaction, we can gain subtle clues as to how those we interact with want to be interacted with, what they are looking for and why, and how to manage ourselves in these exchanges. In fact, using these tools, you will become aware enough so that the impulsive pull to engage on autopilot can be better managed.

Before we begin, let us consider our role in the process of our most common human interactions. Most of us believe that if we "sell" ourselves and do a good job of convincing a person that we are a worthy person, we can quickly have better relationships. If we do not have the experience we are looking for, we wonder what we may have missed or blamed others for the lack of affirmative response. Afterwards, we play Monday morning quarterback and think about a new strategy or evaluate where it went awry. In this process, we never consider the drive of the other person and their connection to us or, better yet, our role in this process beyond the obvious.

Through this Insight-related clinical relationship approach, you can learn how to better understand what is transpiring in your interactions with others and increase your percentage of favorable outcomes. The funny thing is that it does not come from looking outside but inside. This is easy for me to say, or write for that matter, but it really can be this simple. Simplicity is actually harder than it looks, for it means we need to let go of the supposition that our interactions are about our presentation and less about ourselves. I am not talking about an image within the stereotypical relationships, but more about how we present as individuals. This has much to do with you having a genuine interest in the person you are speaking with and one's own autopilot.

Ok, so I laid the groundwork and yet told you nothing about how we do this. Hmm? Let's do a little education about some clinical concepts first so we can begin the process.

Transference

Transference is a key concept of systematic coaching and an essential modality in the context of human relationships. Martyn Carruthers wrote that transference emerges, along with counter-transference and transference loops, in the context of many interpersonal situations. He developed ways to dissolve transferences between partners, family members, and teams.

In our desire to resolve these issues, we reenact the previous experiences within the new relationship to get a resolution. This means that we tend to transfer previous experiences onto people who play the role or remind us of people in our past. Simple examples would be not liking someone because they look like someone you knew in the past or trying to get love from someone who reminds you of your childhood sweetheart. Remember, these are subconscious and not known to the person playing it out. This is how it can obstruct relationship approaches, for we may not know we are doing it at the moment. By gaining better clarity of trigger points within, you can transcend this obstruction and get a clearer picture of the situation.

Counter-Transference

Counter-transference is when the therapist begins to transfer the therapist's own unconscious feeling to the patient because of the therapy sessions. For example, a therapist might have a strong desire for a client to get all A's in university because the client reminds her of her children at that stage in life and the anxieties that the therapist experienced during that time. Another example is a therapist who did not receive enough attention from her father, perceiving her client as too distant and resenting him.

This issue can be applied to any relationship where there is a power differential such as doctor-patient, lawyer-client for our unconscious feeling can impact our ability to guide the client via a clear understanding of their particular needs. By knowing our and the other's unconscious motivations, we can more clearly hear what motivation people have in communicating with us.

Attachment Theory

Attachment is an emotional bond to another person. Psychologist John Bowlby was the first attachment theorist, describing attachment as a "...lasting psychological connectedness between human beings" (Bowlby, 1969, p. 194.)

Bowlby believed that the earliest bonds formed by children with their caregivers have a tremendous impact throughout life. According to Bowlby, attachment also keeps the infant close to the mother, thus improving the child's chances of survival.

The central theme of attachment theory is that mothers who are available and responsive to their infant's needs establish a sense of security. The infant knows that the caregiver is dependable, creating a secure base for the child to explore the world.

http://psychology.about.com/od/loveandattraction/a/attachment01.htm

This security is practical because attachment connects to primary needs and can be a powerful tool in the early stages of a crisis. Applying attachment theory to our goals with others at the beginning stages of our interactions can lead us to better results as we can better assess our goals versus the others. For example, if you were not given the security early on of a present parent, your insecurities on loss can make you seem needier to the other person and vice versa. It does not mean this is permanent, but you need to be aware of it.

Object Relations

Object relations is a modern adaptation of psychoanalytic theory that places less emphasis on the drives of aggression, sexuality, and motivational forces and more focus on human relationships as the primary drivers in life. As Freud suggested, object relations theorists believe that we are relationship-seeking rather than pleasure-seeking. The importance of relationships, in theory, translates to relationships as the focus of psychology, especially the relationship with the therapist.

Freud initially used the term "object" to mean anything an infant directs drives toward for satisfaction. Drives are of two types: libidinal and aggressive. Accordingly, objects became a key component of Freud's drive/ structural model of the human psyche. Since Freud, however, many theorists such as Klein, Fairborn, Wincing, Jacobson, Kernberg, and Kohl have moved, in varying degrees, toward a relational/structural model of the psyche in which an "object" is the target of relational needs in human development.

Modern object relations theorists believe that humans have an innate drive to form and maintain relationships. This fundamental human need forms a context against which other drives, such as libidinal and aggressive drives, gain meaning. The interplay of our drives can manifest themselves in our general interaction with others with the play out in our reality. Similar to transference, but more focused on our drives to survive. One could be living a pattern of abuse whose origins stem from early object relation deficits such as lack of consistent nurturing from their primary caregiver.

https://en.wikipedia.org/wiki/Object_relations_theory

Jungian Archetypes

This may seem like a lot to absorb. Still, there are many different applications of these principles to your interactions with the outside world, best described as intuitive knowing. Malcolm Gladwell wrote about the incredible microprocessor called the human mind. Unlike a computer, it works on many levels computing at high speeds from the many sensory input devices such as the five senses. He went further to say that intuitive knowing is a process that can be harnessed and utilized to work on assimilation without "trying" to figure it out.

As it directly relates to Jungian archetypes, The most common type one sees in a clinical setting are the hero, the healer, the warrior, the martyr, and the caregiver. There are many more, so it does help to know what your motivation is in direct interaction with another person. When thinking of ways to best interact with others, it is always helpful to know what you seek to gain from said relationship. This insight is essential in knowing how we relate to the world and whether our intentions, overt or covert, impact us in our relationship with others. Or better yet, how it triggers reactions by others that may have unintended consequences. We will look at these concepts in more detail in later chapters, but these are the basic concepts for your edification.

CHAPTER TWO

Intuitive Knowing

Intuitive Knowing + Clinical Understanding = Increased Insight

Intuitive knowing is the process of using our minds to do more than we can explain at any given time. It is the instinct that leads us through situations via an autopilot-like guidance system for most of us. I am sure you can think of a time where after a threatening event, you said to yourself, "I do not know how I was able to manage that crisis, but I remember everything slowing down." Were you really able to slow things down? Or, did your intuitive self, aka your Brain kick into overdrive and processed the information quicker than you ever did before?

This idea is not a simple concept to grasp, but it has its origins in the concepts discussed earlier. In essence, when we let go of our physical self, we become fluid in thought and action. It is analogous to the blindfolded marksmen who can shoot with pinpoint accuracy. This is accomplished by actually letting go of the external world and accessing it using internal mechanisms.

As a personal example, when I decided to study the Contra (standup) bass, I took lessons from an eccentric teacher, who told me that before I started with him, I needed to read the book "Zen in the Art of Archery." I was surprised at this request and outwardly protested because it did not make sense to read about archery when I was attempting to learn a musical instrument.

After I consented, I sat down and read about the duality of consciousness and its connection to the physical plane. In essence, the marksmanship needed for archery had a significant connection to playing a fretless instrument. The ability to focus your mind's eye on a target while letting go of the pain induced by the physical plane forces a duality of being. To hit a target, the mind and body work with and against each other for one cause. This requires a disconnect from the physical self to support the goal of achievement.

We become the observer of the physical self, a puppeteer, if you will, that allows us to accomplish what we set out to do. It does not have to be a crisis to access it, just letting go of self. The paradox is that we need both the physical and intuitive selves to accomplish it.

In essence, the resistance points in the physical world give us insight into what we need to work on in our emotional bodies. This ultimately frees our minds to access the intuitive self. Yoga is another great example of the duality of pain and observed consciousness.

Another nice example of the human mind's power was also connected to a musical event. There was a time when I was an adolescent and was practicing an arduous passage in a tune called Boogie's Blues. No matter how hard I tried, I could not get the turn around on the fourth string and stumbled every time I played it. What happened was not something I planned on doing but accidentally stumbled upon. One night I had a dream, and in this dream, I practiced this passage repeatedly until I learned the technique. What made this amazing to me is that when I woke up, the first thing I did was walk over to my instrument, and all that I learned in my dream was retained, and I was able to play the passage.

Here is another hint about letting go and allowing our supreme computer to work on problems without our physical interference. In a book I read in high school, titled "Grokking", a stranger in a strange land, of course, I am not claiming that this skill is easy to access regularly but know through experience that if you apply this understanding to your interaction with people and human relationships, etc., the world slows down. Problems become an opportunity for solutions that are offered to you without interference. In fact, it is the exact opposite of what you were taught in school. Knowledge is handed to you in a moment of clarity, not by forcing things or the act of thinking.

CHAPTER THREE

Increased Insight

Clinical Knowing + Intuitive Knowing = *Increased Insight*

Ok, so now we took an in-depth look into ourselves concerning intuitive knowing and clinical understanding, but how to put the two together? Well, the good thing here is that they are dependent upon each other in that once you start increasing awareness of clinical understandings, you automatically begin to gain access to intuitive knowing. Your ability to empathize with others through your past experiences becomes a standard for how you interact with others and yourself. Freud talks about the subconscious and how once you tap into a repressed memory or experience it via psychoanalysis, it is virtually impossible to ignore it.

For example, once you know the unconscious meaning behind your motivation within an interpersonal action, it is tough to ignore it in the future. Of course, many cannot stay in this place of insight, for it harbors many demons and fears, so they choose to squash the feelings using a series of defense mechanisms. The most commonly known one is denial.

Let us look at a few of these. They follow the levels of emotional evolution, the highest being sublimation, which is a very sophisticated but often misdiagnosed mechanism. These were formulated by Freud's daughter, which given her dad, might have been incredibly aware of all of them. Hopefully, she did not have to deal with them one by one.

In essence, all of these connect to man's evolutionary stages. As we move through the evolutionary hierarchy, you can see how they connect to a purposeful and realistic need to survive in a world. At one time, the world was an incredibly hostile and harsh environment that did not allow man to have the leisure time to think about the "why," for it would only hinder the ability to survive.

When we think of Maslow's pyramid, we can plug in the corresponding defense mechanisms that connect to them. This is an overgeneralization but should give better insight into behavior.

Repression

Repression is the use of keeping unwanted thoughts and feelings from awareness. This may include memory loss of specific events, especially traumas. There are many gradations of these, ranging from simply forgetting a traumatizing event at the age of five to forgetting the content of an argument with your wife earlier in the day. However, you are conscious of forgetting or just not remembering it. Others may not be connected to emotional injury but not tap into those feelings.

Reaction Formation

Reaction Formation is similar to repression. It involves keeping out of awareness certain impulses, such as being overly nice when you actually want to express unacceptable anger at someone. Sarcasm can be a type of reaction formation. I had an experience with a client who was not very nice, and the more she demeaned and belittled me, the kinder I got. I kept doing the opposite the more insulting she got with me, which was counter-intuitive, for I was unable to set boundaries and found myself not feeling like my best self afterwards.

Projection

Projections are when an individual attributes unacceptable thoughts and feelings to others that they have themselves but are unaware they exist. This is a lower-level defense but can manifest in higher functioning people at any given time. You may meet a person telling you things like you need to do better when they themselves need to work on it. I had an experience with a boss who harped on me for being tardy when he was always late for work. In fact, he was so late all the time that he could not gauge about what time I came to work, for he was never there on time to know.

Isolation

Sometimes referred to as "isolation of affect," isolation is when the feelings associated with specific content are repressed but are expressed in another event. For instance, a young man may not be able to cry about the loss of his mother, but he weeps uncontrollably when he sees the same loss on television.

Regression

Regression involves returning to a previous level of functioning or behavior to avoid feelings associated with an event. A child may lose bladder control after their parents' separation long after being toilet trained. Independent people may become exceptionally clingy after a breakup.

Denial

Denial is the purposeful negation or lack of acceptance of important aspects of the reality of one's own experience. A person may deny the existence of pending loss, for it is too painful to experience.

Sublimation

Sublimation is considered one of the highest defense levels because it involves altering what is socially unacceptable to a more socially acceptable form. It can be both positive and negative depending on the particular use. In fact, all the defenses have positive and negatives and can bring temporary solace in a given traumatic event. For instance, the film American Gangster has the protagonist giving out turkeys to the community when he is hurting them by selling drugs to the youth of the same community. It is when it becomes fixed and maladaptive when it hinders insight.

Insightful Empathy Oriented Approaches to Relationships

So why is this important for insightful empathy-oriented approaches to relationships?

Well, in a given transaction between you and another person, any or all of these can be present. By knowing which ones, you are working with, you can better understand which ones are yours and which ones belong to the others. Suppose you are in a situation where you are overly friendly to a client when you would rather yell at them. In that case, you are most likely experiencing a personal defense that influences the interaction, which may ultimately be felt by the other person as insincere or fake.

On the other hand, you may be finding that the person is overtly angry with you when you did nothing to provoke them. Once we differentiate between them and us, we can use this unconscious material to understand better need and want and how best to overcome it and move to a better understanding of what the individual is really saying and therefore help them get there.

Or, you might also be able to cut your losses quicker by not spending time with a person who is using the interaction to play out early narcissistic injury, which can be resolved by giving them what they need versus what they say they want but requires a lot of time and attention.

This higher level of insight relationships can be mastered over time. *When we move to process recordings this material in the activity in Chapter 7, you will become more aware and, therefore, more insightful.*

There is no expectation that you will know every one of these concepts or memorize their definitions, for they are many. We want to get to know ourselves better to understand others better and become more insightful and sincere in genuinely hearing and feeling what others are communicating with us in the transactional dyad.

Maslow's hierarchy in connection to evolutionary need, please see the illustration.

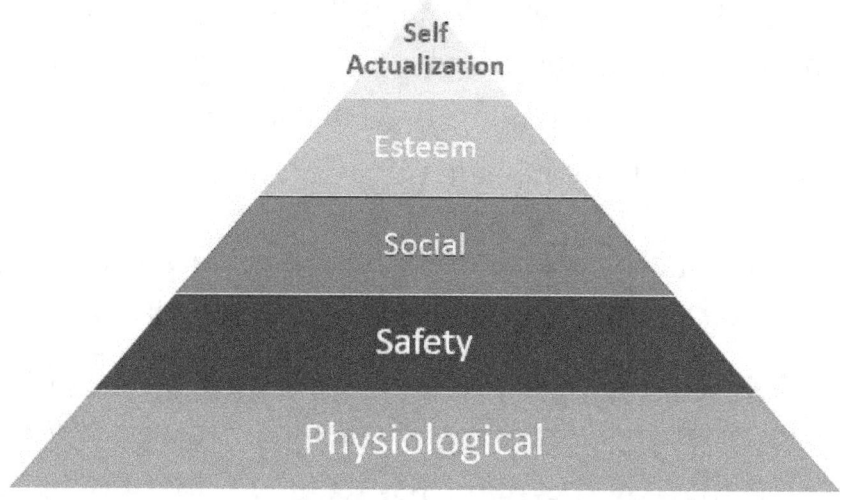

Maslow's Hierarchy of Needs

This is a simplified way to connect how defense mechanisms are connected to the evolutionary hierarchy as set forth by Maslow.

Physiological- Manifested as Repression. Repression for basic needs require that we suppress the pain and hurt to get to the next level, safety. The need to protect our physical self to survive forces the repression of distasteful or traumatic events. This is basic human instinct and basic defense mechanisms.

Safety can be denial or repression, for once, we get past physiological needs, our minds can evolve higher-level tools to protect the self from doing what needs to be done to survive. A simple way to look at it is that if a hunter from 100,000 years ago witnessed the death of a fellow hunter in a previous hunt, he/she would have no choice but to repress or deny previous pain to keep fear from stopping them from hunting again. Without this mechanism, they would perish from starvation.

Social is typically Reaction Formation. You can see this manifest in the Housewife Programs you can see on television. That would make an interesting drinking game by having a sip every time you see reaction formation in action. Remember, this can be overtly kind or Sarcasm when you rather be yelling at someone.

Esteem can be Reaction Formation and all the above for they protect the self from unwanted emotional pain or hurt.

Self-Actualization can be Sublimation for its highest level that can include many others. In fact, they may all be interwoven into how we function; even the greatest people on the planet had these built into their functionality. It does not mean they are bad. It just means that you are human. The path to self-actualization means we always have work to do to make sure we do not become oblivious to these mechanisms

CHAPTER FOUR

Physical Knowing

Using the concepts we discuss in the first chapter, we can see how our bodies react emotionally to other beings through their projections of feelings, transference, or our own developed reactions to situations or perceived situations. They can fall into two categories transference and countertransference.

Counter-transference

What is the other person thinking, needing, wanting, and why? By developing a knowledge of who we are and what causes us to react a certain way in a given situation, we can better assess our client's need or interpersonal interaction. Obviously, in one sitting, we cannot accomplish what people spend a lifetime trying to discover about themselves, either with psychoanalysis or study of the craft. But we can become more aware of our physical reactions and thereby become better listeners by assessing our physical responses.

Let's look at the term Transference again because this is one of the essential concepts I want to establish. Transference is directly connected to the needs and wants of those we engage with. In a social interaction or phone discussion, we can feel the need of the person with whom we are communicating. When we speak of the clinical interpretation of this concept, we begin to unveil what people need. We want to use our feelings through knowing the difference between what is our "stuff" (Intuitive and clinical knowing) and their "stuff."

By knowing our places of unresolved conflict through accessing the body's impulse to act; differently, we can increase the number of people with whom we sincerely connect. For example, suppose we are trying to convince someone of what might be best for them, and the person subconsciously reminds us of a person in our past. In that case, we will never be able to move past the desire to reenact our previous relationship.

Let's look at it from the other perspective. I am sure you have been in situations where the person you are engaging with did not seem to connect to you at all and that they felt as though they were working on a different agenda than you. This lack of connection does not instill confidence but alienates us. This is what we are trying to stop via accessing our body's signals.

Transference

Think of a moment where you reacted to a situation, and afterward, you realized that maybe your reaction was more intense because of another circumstance or personal interaction. In other words, you may have displaced your frustration or anger onto someone else. Well, this is transference in a nutshell. Your reaction to the person or circumstance was more connected to your personal experience and feelings projected onto the other person than the actual situation. When we begin to filter out our stuff, what is left is the other person's stuff. This is what we want to use. Our understanding of our physical and emotional reactions becomes a filtration device to hear the need and want of the other, for that matter.

I would imagine that there were situations where you had a person say to you, "No thanks, I am not hungry," when you knew they were not telling you the truth.

How did you know? Was it the way they said it? On the other hand, was it a feeling you had? Or maybe, it was their body language? If you happened not to be hungry, you would be more apt to believe them and miss the opportunity to get an accurate snapshot of what the person was saying.

In any of these cases, the only way you can truly "feel" the truth is not to be filled with your personal feelings but aware of how the other person acts and transfers. This is much like this concept, but you need to remain aware, or better yet, let go of your stuff so you can hear and feel the other. It is the suspension of self or a neutral observance. This isn't easy for you to achieve, look at your agenda while also letting it go. This is the duality we discussed in the first chapter.

CHAPTER FIVE

Increased Empathy

Now we will add another element to the picture, for once we add physical knowing into the equation, we cannot go back. Our lives will be different. Our abilities lead us to a responsibility to use them for the better good of both parties. Knowing when we are pushing our agenda, and they are pushing theirs, or should I say the give and take of any transaction or interaction, we become more aware. Things will slow down at the moment of the transaction, for the depth of the communication is deeper and more meaningful for both parties.

This depth increases awareness related to Insight and our physical body's reaction to the moment. The five W's come to mind as we do this dance, back and forth, between our needs and their needs. What, when, where, why and who? Our line of questioning moves away from the give and take of the moment, but more importantly, moves to what is really being communicated by the other person and ourselves.

When you ask a question, how do you feel? How do they react? How does this affect you, and why? The questioning becomes deeper. The listening becomes more intense. The communication is clearer. This will show up in other areas of your life. As you continue to practice this skill, your awareness will be more present with each insightful interaction.

Those who you interact with will truly hear you. Not because you are trying to convince them of something, but because you give them a blank slant to express what they need and crave.

This can only lead to more satisfaction by both parties and a more meaningful relationship overall. Of course, this will increase positive experiences and improve the satisfaction of your interactions with them. This is an intangible skill set that many companies spend millions trying to achieve. The irony here is that it does not require anything more than knowing ourselves.

The caveat here is that this is not an easy thing to do, and I am sure many of you will shy away from looking at varying aspects of yourself and frankly give up. I implore you to think about the fact that you are not giving up on this concept but more likely giving up on yourself. Many people cannot even begin to grapple with these concepts, and they have been doing clinical work for years. I do not expect anyone to do this without hard work and dedication to better relationships. The by-product of which is the increased positive relationships, and better understanding as to why it's better

Now, I am hesitant to throw in my success in relationships with these concepts, but I ask you to trust that they work. I can say this much. I took a start-up branch for a niche company that had all odds against it and made it profitable within one year and have doubled year in and year out ever since. Our employees and referrals come almost exclusively by word-of-mouth, and the upside potential is still high. How did I do this? By learning to listen to myself and the other person actively

CHAPTER SIX

Spiritual Knowledge

There is a very simple word that runs rampant in spirituality and faith: trust. Webster's definition of faith is "acceptance of the truth of a statement without evidence of investigation." This concept is trendy today in the writings of prominent spiritual leaders such as Deepak Chopra and a significant component of this training manual.

Now, this is tough to play out in the reality of the now. How can one trust what one does not see? How can we believe the reality of an alternate experience that runs parallel to what we see and hear? Many of my colleagues ask me how I know of something. Did you use a formula or a system? My answer is usually no, and you can see their faces change, trying to hide the feeling of doubt. Still, for the most part, when it comes to human nature, we can be correct in understanding the truth if we believe without investigation.

Aristotle spoke of accessing information already known. We need to give ourselves permission to use traditional means of education which are rote and prescribed. Yet, in actuality, we are relearning it! This is the truth and trust of the spiritual knowledge. We need to accept it. Otherwise, it becomes something else. Influences such as external value systems and parental and cultural impact can alter our ability to trust, creating a conflict. Many of my clinical supervisor's struggle with this basic concept. If you are true to your empathic self of treating others as yourself, you will never stray from what is ethically correct. This leads to a greater knowledge of the person you want to get to know because, in essence, we all have the same needs. You just need to know they are the same.

Trust in the knowledge base is essential for spiritual knowledge, for it drives us through our subconscious. The harboring of truth lies within the infrastructure of the collective. Our experiences in our history are collected and stored, therefore used when we want to use them. Love, hate, patterns of abuse, loss, all reactions are stored and can be accessed.

Ask a specific question to those you engage with. They will enlighten you about their inner knowing, and you can access their spiritual knowledge. This is not to be confused with values and general indoctrination of culture, religion, and life. The best access to this true self is by asking about a specific event in their lives that was traumatic or life-threatening. This is where the true self reveals itself. Many men and women develop a relationship in wars that lasts their lifetimes. Why is this true? While they are at death's door, trusting the other person for survival, their true self arrives, and the spiritual knowing reveals itself in action.

This is why all aspects of the previous chapters are essential, for they combine to give you the answer you are looking for in what the person truly wants and what you want as well. Paring some of the false presentations of self through the previous selection leads us to the answer… "What do they want from you?" Safety and security are the cornerstones of what most people are looking for. When reviewing marketing materials for car manufacturers. You will see them angling toward areas of safety when it comes to those that value family or speed for the jet-set, or both, for that matter.

The key to spiritual knowledge is to tap into the esoteric self in that we need to ask questions that lend themselves to the core of knowing. In other words, I may present as a generous, devil-may-care person, but in reality, I could be a scared, insecure person. Will knowing that gain access to the question? How can you help me? If you can turn off your desire to convince others of your worth and turn on your desire to understand, you are more likely to have better, more consistent relationships. You will spend more time listening intently and asking the right questions instead of trying to "sell" yourself to the wrong person. Remember, if you spend time on a person that is unlikely to listen, you lose time on other possible relationships.

Lately, I have been applying this method to my practice and see that what is presented and what is being are two different things. I had a client once yell at me for 20 minutes, and despite my attempts to intercede, I was left just to listen. When she finally calmed down enough for me to talk and ask a few questions, she told me that she was actually very angry with her phone company for charging her an extra 3 dollars a month and lost trust in them based on her experience. It is hard to trust that the circumstance is not about us in a situation like this. So, I found myself wanting to defend the indefensible since it had nothing to do with me. If I was to argue back, I would have never found out what she was really peeved about and would have just argued back and forth without there ever being a resolution. Trusting the quieter voice deep inside me was essential to access spiritual knowledge, for it falls in line with faith. In essence, hearing has many levels, and knowing what is yours and what is theirs is part of this process.

CHAPTER SEVEN

Pulling It Together

Now that we have traveled through a basic understanding of what makes people stick; now we need to use that to help us access others. We have touched upon the concepts of transference, counter-transference, defense mechanisms, and other areas that influence people's interaction with each other. Now we need to know how to access them. What questions do we ask and when? How can we put this together without seeming mechanical or losing focus in the process?

This is where we start to think of the paradox of accessing others, for the true answer is in accessing ourselves. This is what I call the inner dialog. The inner dialog is the conversation we have with ourselves in trying to engage with others. It is the place where we "try" to guide other people by engaging and understanding their needs. In fact, we need to listen intently to what we are feeling and saying and filter out our own fears and inhibitions, ascertaining what is ours and what is their stuff. The best way to achieve this is through a process recording approach.

Process Recording

One of the most important skills to develop true listening skills is self-reflection. The processing recording as a tool helps guide the acquisition of this skill. It helps you focus on your thoughts, beliefs, actions, and reactions in relation to practice. Good use of this will capture the various facets of a relationship's moment and identify what you did well and where improvement is needed. The tool will address and examine both the content and the interaction process with the relationships system.

The objectives of the tool are:

- To structure thinking about personal practice
- To conceptualize what happens in the transactions between the relationships and the other person's operating system.
- To heighten awareness of oneself in the interaction as part of a transaction

-   To distinguish facts from judgments and impressions

You determine the setting or practice movement, though you should select events that will improve insight and feedback on your practice. It is suggested that the tool help address learning areas, as identified by you or your supervisor.

The tool should be turned in to your supervisor for review and comment.

Directions/Format (Example on page 71)

Cover page

Put your name on the upper left-hand corner, with the date of the meeting below your name

Setting

Describe the place in which this interaction occurred

-   Why did you select this interaction?

Background

- (Be sure to change any identifying characteristics to maintain anonymity): provide general age of the client, race, gender, and any other information that might be useful without disclosing the identity.
- Indicate how often you've seen this client and in what capacity or context.

Purpose of This Interaction

- You are seeing this client for a professional reason
- What is that? What goals do you have for this interaction?

Tuning In

What are you expecting or anticipating? (Describe your thoughts and feelings before the interaction)

- Put information verbatim into the columns as you best remember so your coach can review it.
- Recreate all or part of the actual interaction (should be at least 15 minutes.)
- You should write this as soon as possible after the actual interaction. Be as precise as you can in terms of verbal and nonverbal communication. You

cannot tape record for these lessons. Summarize any parts of the interaction not included in step 2 (i.e., The remainder of this session.)

Impressions and Analysis

What was your overall impression of the interaction?

- How do you understand the other person's situation and behavior?
- Briefly characterize your role(s) in the transaction
- Indicate what intervention skills were and were not useful
- Did you achieve your purpose/goals? Why or why not?

Overall Assessment

- How effective were you?
- What can you improve on for next time?
- Plan/contract for future interactions
- What have you and the client contact decided to work on?
- Indicate next steps

Final Pointers

It is important to remember what you communicated (verbally and nonverbally). Your ability to recall will improve in time. Remember, the focus is on you, the relationships person, not the other way round.

- Perfect practice is not expected, so do not write this up in the manner that edits out your true self. You are writing honestly about this interaction, not writing a work of fiction. We all make mistakes, which are essential to our learning and professional development.
- Be sure to leave room throughout (such as wide margins) for comments from your supervisor or confidant. Your leader or trained professional should review and provide feedback before you submit the process recording to your field liaison.
- Proofread your paper. Make sure it says what you intended. Think about clarity.

Please do this exercise three times on your next three interactions, so you start to understand how this works.

Ok, hopefully now you are back. Did you learn anything about the difference between what you are experiencing and what your client is experiencing? Did you see that your fears and their fears were different? The key is to start to filter out yourself from the equation and home in on what they are experiencing. This can be done using process recording.

I remember a time when I was selling the obligatory vacuum cleaners. Of course, it was a short venture killed by the following event. Still, it gave me insight into how this works on a relationship level. I went on a relationship call back in the '90s and, at the time, was having difficulty selling the product. I intended to get a sale and had a strong intention to sell. I got to the address to do my demonstration that was set up to create fear and horror while claiming how our product would change this fear to safety and security. I do not want to give too much away about this presentation for fear of being sued, but it was pretty much a standard in the industry. But I digress.

When I arrived at the house, I realized it was a trailer and was horrified when I saw that the rug was a loosely scattered array of yarn which was once a shagged rug. I knew my presentation would be a disaster because the carpet was a big part of the pitch. It was at that moment that my fear led to an overarching calm. It created a sense of peace because I was destined to fail, so I might as well make the best of it. I let go of my obstruction and connected to the place of knowing. I listened intently to their fears and let the presentation be what it needed to be. In essence, I stopped trying and started being.

This is a Zen concept but is very useful in relationships in that just as we can sense others, others can sense us.

As presented in many car-dealer showrooms, a false sense of confidence is one of the biggest turn-offs in the market today. Many people laugh about it, but the method stays the same.

Car Dealer – "Hey, can I help you find something?"

Customer – "No thanks, just looking."

Car Dealer – "We have many new cars here on the lot. What price range are you looking for?"

Customer – "Between $6000 and $9000."

Car Dealer – "We do not have that many in that price range, but we do have some good ones starting at $9000."

And on and on it goes. The first problem here is that the dealer is already pushing people out of their comfort zone and not listening to them. This is where they begin to lose many customers. Although it may appear that they are filtering out those that will not buy, they are losing out on potential satisfied customers who could be long-term loyal customers.

CHAPTER EIGHT

Accessing Self

We have to look out into the world and see if we listen well to "the other" the potential for positive relationships is a given. But this is only part of the equation. We now need to listen to ourselves, for this is where we truly get to hear what the person wants and is not saying.

Through transference mentioned earlier, we can now begin intuitive listening and almost appear to read the person's mind to understand their needs better and wants. Through this customized understanding, we can tap into a resource that will build our reputation as fair and supportive while increasing the amount of positive outcomes via deeper engagement with others. In turn, this reduces pressure on you and increases motivation for our engagement in relationships and, of course, ourselves.

So, let's begin looking at how we access this place. Remember the process recordings you did in the previous chapter. Well, this is the beginning of your new awareness and understanding of how to access yourself to connect better with others. In the process, your reaction to internal dialogue exists while talking with another person. This is the dialog we will look at more in-depth now.

When guided by this internal dialog, we are also working on filtering out your personal agenda from the other's needs. This can be very tricky, and you truly need to focus on your part to improve upon this skill.

First, when looking at your internal dialog, try to see if there is a connection to your past or an agenda to resolve. This can be helpful if you keep doing your process recordings and analyzing them. As such, you start filtering your needs from the others and begin to find out what they are genuinely asking. Sounds hard, I know, but it takes practice. Successful people learn from their mistakes and have this heightened skill as part of a successful relationships person. But this is something that can be learned.

We are not suddenly trying to figure out what other people may want by using this skill. We learn from them by filtering our needs and accessing them in complete totality.

CHAPTER NINE

Putting It All Together

So, this has been an interesting introspective experience that teaches us to be better listeners by filtering out our own objections and accessing our true relationship potential by understanding how to best give them what they need and therefore gain trust and interconnectedness. In addition to which, we can now use this material to increase positive interactions with other people while also learning where it may not be best to pursue relationships given what we now know about ourselves.

The first step is to get a better clue as to what is truly transpiring in the situation when we meet a person. Remember the equation: Intuitive knowing + clinical understanding = increased relationships. Socialization is how sincerely we present ourselves. Clinical understanding is how we tap into the needs of the person we are engaging with. And the increased relationships come from the combination of the two aspects. But how?

Let's say a person inquires about who you are and what you can do for them. Most of the time, we want to launch into a pitch about ourselves and what we can do for them without finding out what they need first. How many times have you walked away from a situation when you felt like no one was listening or the agenda seemed to be against your better wishes?

The customer knows best what they can afford (emotionally, monetarily, and intellectually) and their financial situation, and they should be part of the process. This understanding can lead to trusting the relationships person, which is essential in relationships (attachment theory.) We spend too much time looking for the quick fix when we can better grow our relationships and feed our appetites for life. You know that adage about teaching a man to fish, and he eats for a lifetime. This applies here as well.

I have often taken consultations, listened intently to the client's needs, and pushed forth what we can offer only when it applies to their situation. This fills in two needs.

1) The client sees how our approach and skills relate to their situation (removal of transference issues)

2) Shows the client that we truly listen and care (attachment theory, Jungian archetypes)

This cannot be done insincerely. I caution you to use it to help connect with other people and increase your successful relationships. Use it for the wrong reason, and people will turn on you. They will feel manipulated and be more likely to see you from a negative perspective.

This, in essence, is the paradox of this method. You need sensitivity to the other person's needs and to let go of the potentiality of your approach that does not fit who you really are. Use the time to educate and engage with them and their needs as well as yours.

Apple has done a great job of using this approach, for they only cater to the right customer and do not spend time educating those that do not need their products. This creates fierce loyalty through listening to the potential customers in the industry and guiding them with your newly acquired listening skills.

A Test in Time

Early on, my experiences with those that lacked empathy created frustration and some anger with me. In context, it made no sense as to why someone could not see from beyond their own view of the world. Projecting out their insecurities and fears onto others while fostering a deeper relationship built on trust was not exactly the best approach to develop an empathetic interaction. Given these situations, it became a competition to get one's own needs met that created barriers to knowing the wants and needs of each other. It's a literal sword fight that leads to emotional injury, hurt, and or just alienation. A clinical environment is a rich place for this type of interaction. As a manager of clinical and sales associates, I have applied the principles above to help them understand how they could potentially be creating the exact opposite of their desired effect at the moment of first getting to know someone.

Defense in Action

In one example, I was sitting in a room with a client, and the salesperson and the client had issues with her mom and felt compelled to help her. Her mom was resistant to help, and this client needed assistance. Her memory was pretty much gone, so her daughter was concerned. As the daughter continued to share her situation and needs, the salesperson kept feature dumping. He talked about all the things he could do for them that were completely unrelated to what was needed. In addition, the fact that he did not listen to the story, observe the body language and learn the latent communication emanating from the person created even more tension in the room. Helpless to remove himself from his predicament his defense system activated even more. He started to wax on and on about the features which made him feel more secure, despite seeing the obvious transpire before him. Needless to say, the client left with a "Don't call me, I will call you" response.

Afterwards, in my debriefing session with the salesperson, we reviewed the circumstances. We replayed all aspects of the interaction from seating arrangements, posture reactions (body language), and internal dialog that led to his decision. As he reflected on my observations, he detected the exact moment that his defenses kicked in. But more importantly, he saw his role in creating the client's defensiveness in the first place. It was the first impression. As the client tried to share intimate and personal issues and experiences with him, he kept giving rote responses that led her to share less and less (resistance), close her posture (latent communication) and become overly nice (reaction formation.) On his part, his fear of acceptance (attachment theory), overcompensation, and counter-transference onto this client made her emotionally locked. She could no longer share anything personal with him so that we could help her. All of this happened silently in a room where it looked like a conversation about a need for service transpired, and we were just parting after a friendly get-to-know-you conversation.

The positive around this was how the salesperson was able to reflect on what they did, how they did it, and what they needed to do differently. He saw the need to develop empathy using active listening skills, connection to internal self as an indicator of when to do the opposite of what he felt compelled to do in the moment of insecurity. Like a trigger point in the massage, he was able to identify his stuck points and places of internal vibration. Then he could move toward the anxiety to ask questions, remain quiet, and let the emotionality move past. So, he could stay present at the moment to deepen the purpose of the interaction by deepening his understanding of the other person's needs versus their wants.

Feeding a Purpose

In another situation, I was working with a less skilled salesperson who was working with a client who called and needed service in the community and how his wife was having difficulty at home. He stated he needed to meet with her immediately to discuss a plan to get service in the home. The salesperson quickly jumped in and met the client at diner to discuss the plan. The client spent 2 hours with the salesperson, where he discussed the history and concerns in great detail. At the end of the meeting, the potential customer told the salesperson that he felt much better after the meeting. He thought that we could assist. He stated he would call back in a week to set up services.

A week later, the salesperson called him back with no response. She was disheartened and reached out to me to discuss what went on. At the moment, I could tell that she helped reduce his anxiety by giving him a voice for his concerns which reduced his desire to act. In essence, she absorbed his anxious projection about his situation, therefore, resolved his problem. Her role in this dynamic was her counter-transference and a caretaker for her family, which given my neutrality, released this, for I have known this about her in our work together in the past. She used this nurturing aspect of herself to offset her feelings of inadequacy when it came to taking care of her parents. This was a driver for her success.

Two weeks later, the client called again and stated he needed to start care right away and needed to meet with her again. This time they needed to meet in the office after 5:00 pm. Of course, he complied, yet he did not meet with her but called her phone. Once again, he spoke with her for over an hour, discussing the latest issues and that he needed to get care started. When pressed for a start date, the client again backed out and stated he would call back to set up a time to start care.

When she shared that he had reached out to her again, I reminded her of what was evident last time in that she was participating in a psychosocial dance. She denied that this was happening and was convinced that he would start service soon. Of course, he did not reach out, and she started calling him weekly to see when service would start. In short, she was getting her needs met by helping him, and he was getting his needs met by reducing his anxiety at the moment.

This went on for 3 months, and finally, the salesperson came to me stating that she was ready to give up. We discussed how she got involved in this dance and how it fed both of their needs, and if she did not give him what he was looking for by not listening to him, he would simply go away. She agreed and stated she would only ask about setting up services. It was then that he said he was fine and never called her again. A few months later, we closed out the inquiry.

The above examples are just a sample of how this interplay can bring us closer or further away. Still, as we develop our deeper empathetic understanding of our motivations, we can see more clearly the motivations of others and truly assist in getting them what they need versus what they want. In the 2nd example, the salesperson gave the client what he wanted but limited the interaction to only that. Once she gave him what he needed, he no longer wanted to interact with her, for his defense was a denial of his circumstance.

Staying in the Moment

In another experience, I worked with an advanced-level clinician and client with a narcissistic personality disorder. The clinician asked me to come along, for she had to confront a man with a history of anger and frustration about his smoking behavior in a congregate housing setting. The other clients had been complaining that this client had been smoking in a public area and falling asleep on the couch with a lit cigarette which was a fire hazard.

The two of us went upstairs to where the client sat on the couch, laced with varying burn marks. The client's cigarettes were on the table in front of him. The clinician and I sat in front of him, and she began to tell him why we were there. The client quickly interrupted her to state, "I know why you are here. You are here to take my cigarettes away, and I can tell you right now that is not going to happen!" He began to start yelling epithets at the two of the facility operators and us as to why we had no right to tell him what to do, and he had every right to smoke whenever and wherever he wanted.

This threw the clinician off and left her scrambling to defend her position. Obviously, this was going nowhere fast, so I thought about how best to find another avenue to get this discussion on a different path. Using my knowledge of working with a client with such strong defenses, I appealed to his ego by pivoting to asking questions about him. Given that I had not worked with this client, I asked him about what he did for a living previous to being with us. Additionally, I inquired as to what he liked most about his job. He was happy to discuss what he did, for he was an editor for a large publication and took pride in the work he did with them.

I then emphasized how important it must be to have objectivity and intelligence in his work, to which he agreed with incredible pride. With that, I saw our window. Once deescalated, I asked him again why he thought we were there. He got his back up again and said, "You are not taking my cigarettes away!" I responded with, "That's not the question." I asked again and waited.

He sat for a moment and said, "You want to take my cigarettes away." My response was, "Possibly. Why would we want to do that?" He paused and said, "Because I'm smoking in the building." I said, "Yes, that's part of it. Can you think of any other reason why that might be an issue?" Once again, he thought and said, "I fall asleep with the lit cigarettes on this couch." "And why would that be a problem?" I responded." He said, "I could start a fire." "Yes," I said, "and that puts many people at risk."

He then realized that he was putting his friends in danger by doing what he was doing and handed me the cigarettes and said, "Here you go. The last thing I want to do is hurt my friends. I will not smoke in here anymore."

The advanced clinician working with me was shocked. I took the cigarettes from the client and thanked him for being so understanding. And interestingly, he thanked us for intervening.

This is a powerful example of removing the emotional self from the interaction while staying in the here and now to ask the right questions to move through this client's denial about his behavior. Other clinical aspects were at play, such as resistance and ego dystonia. Still, in short, it was just about finding out what mattered to him, which made the change easier.

CHAPTER TEN

Final Thoughts

In reflecting on what we learned or are starting to learn, you may find that the path is not easy. The general principle of "know thyself" is essential in differentiating your issues from others. In every interaction, some or all the defensive mechanisms could play out at any time. If you take the time to do the work to understand your role in this process better, the better off you will be.

Simply put, pay attention to your physical self, for it is an indicator of what may be going on with your client or yourself. If you are feeling anxiety for no reason, maybe the person you are speaking with is anxious. Or, possibly, you are anxious based on your own fears, which can exacerbate a negative interaction with the person you are trying to connect with.

There are many variations in the common clinical dyad related to what could be transpiring. So, being the expert on you as an operating system requires practice to be better at hearing what the other person is trying to say, whether verbally or implied. This will lead to more engagement with those you work with or care about while also fostering improvement in your outcomes, for you are truly "hearing" what they want and/or need to achieve their best self. And for that, your satisfaction in dealing with others will be gratifying and meaningful as you make a difference in how you relate to other people one person at a time. If you feel you want to assist with this process, you can reach out to me via my website, listed in the bio section.

Process recording example

Sample Process Recording - First Year MSW Student

Agency: Department of Social Services   **Client System**: Claudia Jones, age 22, unemployed single mother   **Date**: February 22, 20xx
Presenting Issues: Client was referred to DSS for neglecting her 3-year-old daughter, Mia. Mother has custody of child but has been mandated to receive services.
Purpose of Interview: Fourth interview; follow up interview for mandated client

Content	Skills Used	Gut Reaction	Analysis	Field Instructor's Comments
Student (S): How have things been going this week?		I'm happy to see Claudia again.		
Client (C): OK, I guess. Not much different than last week.				
S: Did you get a chance to check into parenting classes like we discussed last week?			I'm following up on what we talked about last week. I want Claudia to know that what she does is important.	
C: No. This wasn't a good week. I know I promised that I'd make phone calls but Mia got sick and I got so tired being up all night with her. Then I guess I forgot.		She's making excuses.		The "Gut Reaction" column is to record your own feelings, rather than your thoughts about the client's motivations. How did you feel when Claudia said that she didn't make the phone call because her daughter was ill?
S: Well, it does sound like this was a hard week for you. Do you think you can make the calls this week?	Empathizing		I'm showing empathy for the client's situation, but I'm also asking her commitment to follow through this week.	Good idea that empathizing with the client would be helpful here. Based on Claudia's response (verbal and non-verbal), how do you think she heard what you